Animal Worlds

Animals in the house

Sue Barraclough

Heinemann LIBRARY

Little Nippers

www.heinemann.co.uk/library
Visit our website to find out more information about **Heinemann Library** books.

To order:
 Phone 44 (0) 1865 888066
Send a fax to 44 (0) 1865 314091
Visit the Heinemann Bookshop at www.heinemann.co.uk/library to browse our
catalogue and order online.

First published in Great Britain by
Heinemann Library, Halley Court, Jordan Hill,
Oxford OX2 8EJ, part of Harcourt Education.
Heinemann is a registered trademark of Harcourt
Education Ltd.

Editorial: Sarah Shannon and Dave Harris
Design: Jo Hinton-Malivoire and bigtop design ltd
Picture Research: Ruth Blair and Kay Altwegg
Production: Chloe Bloom

Originated by Modern Age
Printed and bound in China by South China
Printing Company

ISBN 0 431 00362 9 (hardback)
10 09 08 07 06
10 9 8 7 6 5 4 3 2 1

ISBN 0 431 00367 X (paperback)
10 09 08 07 06
10 9 8 7 6 5 4 3 2 1

British Library Cataloguing in Publication Data
Barraclough, Sue
   Animals in the house. - (Animal worlds)
   636'.0887
A full catalogue record for this book is available
from the British Library.

Acknowledgements
The publishers would like to thank the following
for permission to reproduce photographs:
Alamy/Ian Thraves p. 6; Alamy/Robert Rickett pp.
11, 22; Alamy/Tina Manley p. 18; Ardea/Jean
Michel Labat p. 13; Bengt Lundberg/naturepl.com
p. 7; Corbis pp. 12, 14, 16, 23; FLPA/David
Hosking p. 20; Foto Natura Stock/FLPA p. 8;
Getty Images/Photodisc pp. 10, 14, 19;
Naturepl.com/Aflo p. 15; Naturepl.com/Ulrike
Schanz p. 9; NHPA/Daniel Heuclin p. 17;
NHPA/Ernie Janes p. 9; NHPA/Stephen Dalton p.
13; Oxford Scientific/Larry Lawfer pp. 4, 5;
Photolibrary.com p. 21.

Cover photograph reproduced with permission
of Corbis.

Every effort has been made to contact copyright
holders of any material reproduced in this book.
Any omissions will be rectified in subsequent
printings if notice is given to the publishers.

The paper used to print this book comes from
sustainable resources.

Contents

3

Animals at home

Some animals live
in our homes.
These animals are
called pets.

Pets need to be looked after. Do you have a pet?

5

Different pets

There are lots of different pets.

Dogs like to be taken out for walks.

Cats like to come and go.

Pets need somewhere
to rest and sleep.

This pet is called a chinchilla.
This one lives in a special house.

zzzzZ

Do you think
the dog and the
hamster look safe
and warm?

Food and water

Animals need to eat
food to stay healthy.

crunch

crunch

Moving around

Dogs and cats like to **run** and **jump**.

Can you point to
a pet that can fly?

13

Making noises

Pets make lots of different noises.

Purrrrr

Can you purr softly like a cat?

14

Woof!

This dog can bark loudly.

Can you squeak like a hamster?

Eek-Eeek!

Playing games

Dogs like to play games.

This hamster likes to play in a special wheel.

Can you see how it pushes the wheel around?

Pet shop

Special shops sell all sorts of toys and treats for pets.

These things are for cats and dogs.

Going to the vet

Pets need regular visits to the vet to stay healthy.

This dog has a cage to keep it safe on the journey.

This vet makes sure the puppy is fit and healthy.

Caring and cleaning

Pets need to be cared for and kept clean.

Bowls and cages need to be cleaned out.

Pets sometimes need to be washed.

Do you think this dog likes having a bath?

Index

Notes for adults

This series supports a young child's knowledge and understanding of their world. The following Early Learning Goals are relevant to the series:

* Find out about, and identify, some features of living things, objects, and events that they observe.

* Develop communication, language and literacy by imitating different animal sounds, and to notice and describe similarities and differences.

These books will help children extend their vocabulary, as they will hear some new words. Since words are used in context in the book this should enable young children to gradually incorporate them into their own vocabulary.

This series investigates a variety of animals by looking at distinguishing features and characteristics and by exploring their different environments.

Follow-up activities:

Encourage children to draw a picture of their favourite pet, and to notice and record any distinguishing features and characteristics.